Quips, Quotes and Funnies

Volume 1

Compiled by Dave Smith

Most of the material in this book has been compiled over a long period of time. Where the author is known, the name is listed. However, many of the sources are unknown. The original authors deserve our thanks.

Published by

Spring Ridge Publishing
P.O. Box 3301
Gainesville, GA 30503
United States of America

ISBN: 145-1-540000

Cover design: David Smith

Scripture Quotations are taken from the Amplified Bible, Copyright © 1954, 1958, 1962, 1965, 1987 by the Lockman Foundation

To Jean,

"For all I'd been blessed with in this life
There was emptiness inside.
I was imprisoned by the power of gold.
With one honest touch you set me free.

If the world stops turning,
If the sun stops burning,
If they tell me love's not worth going thru
If it all falls apart,
I will know deep in my heart
The only dream that mattered had come true,
*In this life, I was loved by you."**

* Words and music by Mike Reid and Allen Shamblin; Epic records (as recorded by Collin Raye)

i

CONTENTS

"A word fitly spoken and in due season is like apples of gold in settings of silver."

Proverbs 25:11 (Amp)

INTRODUCTION

"Did you hear about the Pope getting shot?"

"What?"

"Really, did you hear about the Pope getting shot?" I asked again.

"Now come on, tell the joke...and where did you hear this one?" she replied.

In some ways, that's the story of my life.

It was May of 1981. I had just watched my then-favorite radio-tv announcer, Douglas Edwards, read the news story about Pope John Paul II being shot in Vatican Square. I was struck that this veteran newsman seemed to choke up a bit as he read the report. Working as a local radio DJ at the time, I had come to admire those with the vocal and journalistic talents of Mr. Edwards.

So I walked to the kitchen where my wife was making a sandwich lunch before I headed for WPMH radio. And I opened my mouth.

That exchange taught me something. Never ask a serious question with a common joke opening! If you have a light-hearted temperament like I do, and see the humor in most every situation, you might be treated like "chicken-little" even when the sky really is falling.

But humor is everywhere. You've seen it before. Someone says something perfectly harmless and it strikes you as funny. Someone else makes a remark and it succinctly makes a point - one you wish you had made!

This book is a collection of those kinds of quotes and quips that have passed my way. I wish I had come up with them myself!

Where it was possible, I have listed the source. In some cases, they have become part of the public domain - nobody really knows who to give credit. If I omitted or mis-credited a source or author, please let me know.

Otherwise, ENJOY!

David Smith
Flowery Branch, GA

ATTITUDE

Blessed is he who expects nothing, for he shall never be disappointed.
> \- Benjamin Franklin

Every morning we have to decide if we will innovate or replicate.

The only difference between a rut and a grave is distance and depth.
> \- Mark Sanborn

A smile is contagious – Start an epidemic!

My father gave me the best advice of my life. He said, "Whatever you do, don't wake up at 65 years old and think about what you should have done with your life."
- George Clooney

Far better is it to dare mighty things, to win glorious triumphs, even though checkered with failures, than to take rank with those poor spirits who neither enjoy much nor suffer much, because they live in the gray twilight that knows not victory nor defeat.
- Theodore Roosevelt

Persistence trumps talent and looks every time.
- Aaron Brown

Winning depends on where you put your priorities. It's usually best to put them over the fence.
- Baseball player Jason Giambi

Attitude

Worry is interest paid on trouble before it falls due.
- British educator W.R. Inge

Ability is what you're capable of doing. Motivation determines what you do. Attitude determines how well you do it.
- Lou Holtz

We must have strong minds, ready to accept facts as they are.
- Harry Truman

Laughter is an instant vacation.
- Milton Berle

You have to do something that you love. Work isn't work when you love what you do. If you dread going to the office in the morning and can't wait for the workday to end, you need to seriously rethink your career choice.
- Lou Holtz

The one thing that will guarantee the successful conclusion of a doubtful undertaking is faith in the beginning that you can do it.
- William James

The best mind altering drug is the truth.
- Lily Tomlin

Reach for the stars, even if you have to stand on cactus.
- Susan Longacre

If you aren't fired with enthusiasm, you will be fired with enthusiasm.
>   - Vince Lombardi

The purpose of life is to live a life of purpose.

If the rewards you seek are found in the praise and adulation of others, you are destined for disappointment, because the moment you drop one pass, or lose one game, the cheering stops and the praise goes away.
>   - Lou Holtz

It's the little things that make the big things possible. Only close attention to the fine details of any operation makes the operation first class.
>   - J. Willard Marriott

Evidence is conclusive that your self-talk has a direct bearing on your performance.
- Zig Ziglar

You cannot perform in a manner inconsistent with the way you see yourself.
- Zig Ziglar

If you can do something with your eyes closed, it's time to find something new.
- Kathie Lee Gifford

The brain is a commodity …. Use it to fertilize ideas.
- Elbert Hubbard

The pain of sacrifice is nothing compared to the pain of regret – Seen on a high school athlete's t-shirt

COURAGE

Seize the very first opportunity to act on every resolution you make, and on every emotional prompting you may experience in the direction of the habits you aspire to gain.
                    - William James

The man who goes farthest is generally the one who is willing to do and dare. The sure-thing boat never gets far from the shore.
                    - Dale Carnegie

We need to learn to set the course by the stars, not by the lights of every passing ship
                    - General Omar Bradley

Towering genius disdains a beaten path. It seeks regions hitherto unexplored.

If you want to conquer fear, don't sit at home and think about it. Go out and get busy.
- Dale Carnegie

You gain strength, courage, and confidence by every experience in which you stop to look fear in the face.
- Eleanor Roosevelt

It is the greatest of all mistakes to do nothing because you can only do a little.
- Sydney Smith

Courage

Look at the stone cutter hammering away at his
rock, perhaps a hundred times without as much as a
crack showing in it. Yet at the hundred-and-first
blow it will split in two, and I know it was not the
last blow that did it, but all that had gone before.
- Jacob Riis

Living at risk is jumping off the cliff and building
your wings on the way down.
- Ray Bradbury

Only those are fit to live who are not afraid to die.
- Douglas MacArthur

A hero is no braver than an ordinary man, but he is
brave five minutes longer.
- Emerson

If you don't scale the mountain, you won't see the view.

Who bravely dares must sometimes risk a fall.
              - Tobias G. Smollett

The only time you can't afford to fail is the last time you try.
              - Charles Kettering

Courageous risks are life-giving, they help you grow, make you brave and better than you think you are.
              - Joan L. Curcio

Throughout history, the most extraordinary acts of genius have often come in the depths of turmoil.
              - Lou Holtz

Some have been thought brave because they were
afraid to run away.
            - Ralph Waldo Emerson

Courage doesn't always roar, sometimes it is the
voice that says, "I'll try again tomorrow."

It's choice, not chance which determines your
destiny.

Dance like no one is watching.

EVERYDAY LIFE

If you don't like change, you're going to like
irrelevance even less.
> – Gen. Eric Shinseki, Former U.S.
> Army Chief of Staff

If you don't know where you are going, you might
wind up someplace else.
> - Yogi Berra

About the time one learns to make the most out of
life, the most of it is gone.

Rumor is the only thing that gets thicker as you
spread it.

Never try to teach a pig to sing. It wastes your time, and it annoys the pig.
                    - Paul Dickson

When you aim for perfection, you discover it's a moving target.
                    - George Fisher

Profanity is an effort of a feeble mind to express itself forcibly – (Read on a glass office wall in a wallpaper store at age 10)
                    – Clyde Hughes

Since the November 2008 elections, there have been enough guns sold in America to arm both the armies of China and India.

Tomorrow is often the busiest day of the week.
- A Spanish Proverb

Calmness is the cradle of power.
- Josiah Gilbert Holland

Nothing gives a person so much advantage over another as to remain always cool and unruffled under all circumstances.
- Thomas Jefferson

Repetition is the mother of learning, the father of action, which makes it the architect of accomplishment.
- Zig Ziglar

One of these days is none of these days.
- An English Proverb

A word out of season may mar a whole lifetime.
- A Greek Proverb

The eagle that chases two rabbits at one time will catch neither.
– Ancient Chinese proverb

Obstacles cannot crush me. Every obstacle yields to stern resolve. He who is fixed to a star does not change his mind.
– Leonardo da Vinci

It is said that if you could read all the news across the internet for a single day, you would match that contained in the Library of Congress.

Coveting means I have to have what the haves have.
– Ken Crockett

Bitterness is the offspring of an unhealed wound – whose parents are unforgiveness and time.
– Ken Crockett

If the mountain was smooth, you couldn't climb it.

Beware of little expenses. A small leak will sink a great ship.
- Benjamin Franklin

If they're laughing, they ain't gonna shoot you.
                    - Jimmy Durante

If you're only joking, why does it hurt so bad?

Everything should be made as simple as possible,
but not simpler.
                    - Albert Einstein

To ask someone to do something he is incapable of
doing doesn't make him a better player; it makes
you look like a bad coach.
                    - Lou Holtz

The best thing about the future is that it comes only one day at a time.
- Abraham Lincoln

The key to happiness is having dreams; the key to success is making them come true.
- James Allen

Give me four lines written by any man and I can have him tried as a criminal.
- Cardinal Richelieu

Prepare and prevent instead of repair and repent.

Millions long for immortality who do not know what to do with themselves on a Sunday afternoon.
- Susan Ertz

Overload reminds us of the weight of everyday life. We are overwhelmed, overworked, overcommitted, overanxious, overmatched, and overextended. Our tanks are on empty and we're running on fumes.
- Steve and Mary Farrar

Keep yourself alive by throwing day by day fresh currents of thought and emotion into the things you have come to do from habit.
- John Lancaster Spalding

Know what's most important and give it all you've got.
- Lee Iacocca

The reason a dog has so many friends is that he wags his tail instead of his tongue.

There is no psychiatrist in the world like a puppy licking your face.
> - Ben Williams

A dog is the only thing on earth that loves you more than he loves himself.
> - Josh Billings

If your dog is fat, you aren't getting enough exercise.

Quality is like a path through a dense forest. If you step off the path very far, before you know it, you have no idea where you started. You're lost.
> - Cameron Mitchell, President of
> Cameron Mitchell Restaurants

Home: a place where we're treated best but grumble the most.

Experience comes from what we have done.
Wisdom comes from what we have done badly.
                    - Theodore Levitt

All the world's a stage and most of us are desperately unrehearsed.
                    - Sean O'Casey

Happiness is inward, and not outward; and so, it does not depend on what we have, but on what we are.
                    - Henry Van Dyke

Only a person with a Best Seller mind can write Best Sellers.
- Aldous Huxley

The real art of conversation is not only to say the right thing in the right place but to leave unsaid the wrong thing at the tempting moment.
- Dorothy Nevill

The rate at which a person can mature is directly proportional to the embarrassment he can tolerate.
- Doug Engelbart

Dieting advice: Never eat more than you can lift.

Things do not change; we change.
   - Henry David Thoreau

We're surrounded. That simplifies our problems.
   - Lt. Gen. Lewis Puller

The main dangers in this life are the people who
want to change everything…or nothing.
   - Lady Astor

It takes a really honest person to know the difference
between being tired and just plain lazy.
   - Lifelines

No man ever climbed a hill by looking at it.

If everyone is thinking alike then somebody isn't thinking.
            - George Patton

There are only two ways to live your life. One is as though nothing is a miracle. The other is though everything is a miracle.
            – Albert Einstein

IF DOGS WERE THE TEACHERS, YOU WOULD LEARN STUFF LIKE:

- When loved ones come home, always run to greet them.
- Never pass up the opportunity to go for a joyride.
- Let fresh air and the wind in your face be pure ecstasy.
- When it's in your best interest, practice obedience.
- Let others know when they've invaded your territory.
- Take naps.
- Stretch before rising.
- Run, romp, and play daily.
- Thrive on attention and let people touch you.
- Avoid biting when a simple growl will do.
- On warm days, stop to lie on your back on the grass.
- On hot days, drink lots of water, and lie under a shady tree.
- When you're happy, dance around and wag your entire body.
- No matter how often you're scolded, never hold a grudge! Run right back and make friends.
- Delight in the joy of a long walk.
- Eat with gusto and enthusiasm. Stop when you have had enough.
- Be loyal. Never pretend to be something you're not.
- If what you want lies buried, dig until you find it.
- When someone is having a bad day, be silent, sit close by and nuzzle them gently.

- PreachingNow.com

People are so worried about what they eat between Christmas and the New Year, but they really should be worried about what they eat between the New Year and Christmas.

The real voyage of discovery consists not in seeking new landscapes, but in having new eyes.
– Marcel Proust

FAITH AND AMERICA

Providence has given our people the choice of their rulers, and it is the duty of a Christian nation to select and prefer Christians for their rulers.
> - John Jay, First Chief Justice of the Supreme Court

I fervently invoke the aid of that Almighty Ruler of the Universe in whose hands are the destinies of nations.
> - President James K Polk, 1845

It cannot be emphasized too strongly or too often that this great nation was founded not by religionists but by Christians, not by religions but by the gospel of Jesus Christ.
> - Patrick Henry

Upon these two foundations, the law of nature and the law of revelation (the Bible), depend all human laws.

> \- William Blackstone

We are a religious people and our institutions presuppose a Supreme Being.

> \- William O. Douglas
>   Supreme Court Justice

Can the liberties of a nation be thought secure when we have removed their only firm basis, a conviction in the minds of the people that their liberties are the gift of God?

> \- Thomas Jefferson

We have grown in numbers, wealth and power, as no other nation has ever grown. But we have forgotten God.

> \- Abraham Lincoln

It is the duty of all nations to acknowledge the providence of Almighty God.
- George Washington

We are a Christian people...not because the law demands it, not to gain exclusive benefits or to avoid legal disabilities, but from choice and education; and in a land thus universally Christian, what is to be expected, what desired, but that we shall pay due regard to Christianity?
- From a Report of the Senate Judiciary Committee, January 1853

All scholars shall live religious, godly and blameless lives according to the Rules of God's Word, diligently reading the holy Scriptures the Foundation of Light and truth; and constantly attend upon all the Duties of Religion both public and in secret.
- Yale University
Laws of 1745 (for students)

It is my conviction that the fundamental trouble
with the people of the United States is that they have
gotten too far away from Almighty God.
- President Warren Harding

Statesmen…may plan and speculate for liberty, but
it is Religion and Morality alone, which can establish
the Principles upon which Freedom can securely
stand…
- President John Adams

FOOTBALL WISDOM

The heck with statistics, just win.
                - Terry Bradshaw

The sun doesn't shine on the same dog every day.
                - Steve Sloan

In life, you'll have your back up against the wall
many times. You might as well get used to it.
                - Bear Bryant

I can't believe God put us on this earth to be
ordinary.
                - Lou Holtz

When Herschel Walker was asked how he could carry the football 25 or 30 times in a game, he replied, "It's not that heavy."

You get out of life, and out of football, exactly what you put into it. When a person realizes this and acts accordingly, he is sure to succeed.
                    - Bart Starr

Gentlemen, it is better to have died as a small boy than to fumble this football.
                    - John Heisman

Don't think that the way you are today is the way you'll always be.
                    - Vince Dooley

I don't believe in miracles. I believe in character.
                    - Pat Dye

For when the One Great Scorer comes to mark
against your name, He writes – not that you won or
lost – but how you played the game.
                    - Grantland Rice

I can reach a kid who doesn't have any ability as
long as he doesn't know it.
                    - Bear Bryant

Spectacular achievements are always preceded by
unspectacular preparation.
                    - Roger Staubach

First I prepare; then I have faith.
- Joe Namath

When you know what you're doing, you don't get intercepted.
- Johnny Unitas

I don't care where a man comes from or how he spells his name. All I ask is that he be loyal to Georgia, proud of that jersey, and try like the devil to win.
- Wally Butts

When you win, nothing hurts.
- Joe Namath

Every time a player goes out there, at least 20 people have some amount of influence on him. His mother has more influence than anyone. I know because I play, and I love my momma.
- Bear Bryant

Leadership must be demonstrated, not announced.
- Fran Tarkenton

Either love your players or get out of coaching.
- Bobby Dodd

I retired for health reasons. The alumni got sick of me.
- Frank Howard

GOVERNMENT / POLITICS

Government's view of the economy could be summed up in a few short phrases: If it moves, tax it. If it keeps moving, regulate it. And if it stops moving, subsidize it.
> - Ronald Reagan

Providence has given to our people the choice of their rulers, and it is the duty, as well as the privilege and interest of our Christian nation to select and prefer Christians for their rulers.
> - John Jay (America's first Supreme Court Justice)

No free man shall ever be barred from the use of arms. The strongest reason for the people to retain their right to keep and bear arms is as a last resort to protect themselves against tyranny in government.
> - Thomas Jefferson

The only reason a person would decide to become a
politician is either he's too lazy to work or too scared
to steal.

Religion is the basis and foundation of government.
- James Madison

The government is like a baby's alimentary canal,
with a happy appetite at one end and no
responsibility at the other.
- Ronald Reagan

A government big enough to give you everything
you want is strong enough to take everything you
have.
- Thomas Jefferson

Hold on my friends to the Constitution and to the
Republic for which it stands. Miracles do not cluster
and what has happened once in 6,000 years may not
happen again. Hold on the Constitution, for if the
American Constitution should fail, there will be
anarchy throughout the world.
                        - Daniel Webster

The only difference between a tax man and a
taxidermist is that the taxidermist leaves the skin.
                        - Mark Twain

There is no distinctly Native American criminal
class...save Congress.
                        - Mark Twain

What this country needs are more unemployed
politicians.
                        - Edward Langley, Artist

If you don't read the newspaper you are uninformed, if you do read the newspaper you are misinformed.

> \- Mark Twain

In my many years I have come to a conclusion that one useless man is a shame, two is a law firm and three or more is a Congress.

> \- John Adams

No man's life, liberty, or property is safe while the legislature is in session.

> \- Mark Twain

Few men have virtue enough to withstand the highest bidder.

> \- George Washington

Suppose you were an idiot. And suppose you were a member of Congress. But then I repeat myself.
- Mark Twain

I contend that for a nation to try to tax itself into prosperity is like a man standing in a bucket and trying to lift himself up by the handle.
- Winston Churchill

A government which robs Peter to pay Paul can always depend on the support of Paul.
- George Bernard Shaw

Giving money and power to government is like giving whiskey and car keys to teenage boys.
-P.J. O'Rourke

I don't make jokes. I just watch the government and
report the facts.
- Will Rogers

In general, the art of government consists of taking
as much money as possible from one party of the
citizens to give to the other.
- Voltaire (1764)

America will never be destroyed from the outside. If
we falter and lose our freedoms, it will be because
we destroyed ourselves.

Ballots are the rightful and peaceful successors to
bullets.

INTEGRITY

The remarkable thing about fearing God is that
when you fear God you fear nothing else, whereas if
you do not fear God you fear everything else.
- Oswald Chambers

Power does not corrupt. Power simply empowers
resident corruption.
Clyde Hughes

Those who deny freedom to others deserve it not for
themselves.

To be trusted is a greater compliment than to be
loved.
- George MacDonald

True heroes walk the walk with quiet confidence.
They do the job and then let the job they've done
speak for itself.

          - Lou Holtz

A great man shows his greatness by the he treats
little men.

           – Thomas Carlyle

Let us endeavor to live that when we come to die
even the undertaker will be sorry.

          - Mark Twain

I am in earnest, I will not equivocate, I will not
excuse, I will not retreat a single inch, And I will be
heard.

          – William Lloyd Garrison (Leader
             in the movement to abolish
             slavery in America, 1831)

There's harmony and inner peace to be found in following a moral compass that points in the same direction regardless of fashion or trend.
- Ted Koppel

Truth, like gold, is not less so for being newly brought out of the mine.
- John Locke, 1690

If we value privilege more than principles, we will lose both.

Everyone's life is a compilation of the people he meets, the things he does, and the decisions he makes.
- Lou Holtz

Honesty is the first chapter of the book of wisdom.
- Thomas Jefferson

Most powerful is he who has himself in his own power.
- Seneca

You can tell more about a person by what he says about others than you can by what others say about him.
- Leo Aikman

We thought, because we had power, we had wisdom.
- Stephen Vincent Benet

The real measure of your wealth is how much you'd be worth if you lost all your money.

To sin by silence when they should protest makes cowards of men.

Character is like a tree and reputation like its shadow. The shadow is what we think of it—the real thing is the tree.
                    - Abraham Lincoln

A Chinese Proverb says, "A diamond with a flaw is worth more than a pebble without imperfections."

Reputation is what you are in the light; character is what you are in the dark.

Some people handle the truth carelessly; others never touch it at all.

Fr. Richard John Neuhaus wrote concerning his brush with death some years ago: Life is taken seriously when life is held to account, our lives and the lives of others. The worst thing is not the sorrow or the loss or the heartbreak. The worst thing is to be encountered by death and not be changed by the experience.

Always do more than is required of you.
> – General George Patton

Try not to become a man of success but rather try to become a man of value.
> - Albert Einstein

The bravest sight in the world is to see a great man struggling against adversity.
- Seneca

We often act as though comfort and luxury were the chief requirements of life. What we really need to make us happy is something to give our life for.
– Johnny Hunt

Your dreams and talents may carry you to places your character can't keep you.
– Johnny Hunt

Power doesn't corrupt. It simply exposes resident corruption.
- Clyde Hughes

Integrity

Success is more permanent when you achieve it
without destroying your principles.
- Walter Cronkite

A higher calling brings higher scrutiny.
– Johnny Hunt

Washington warned Americans in his farewell
address to the nation in 1796 against those who
would suggest "that morality can be maintained
without religion...reason and experience both forbid
us to expect that national morality can prevail in
exclusion of religious principle."

I believe that being successful means having a
balance of success stories across the many areas of
your life. You can't truly be considered successful in
your business life if your home life is in shambles.
- Zig Ziglar

49

Reputation is what others think about you; character is what God knows about you.
- Adrian Rogers

I believe that if you aren't prepared to keep your word, you shouldn't give it.
- Lou Holtz

The price of greatness is responsibility.
– Winston Churchill

Those who can accomplish great things on their own often want to take the credit for it. So, God loves to use the lowly underdogs of His kingdom to accomplish great things, because they know they couldn't have done it without Him.
- David Jeremiah

Nearly all men can stand adversity, but if you want to test a man's character, give him power.
- Abraham Lincoln

You have to *be* before you can *do*; and you have to *do* before you can *have* (so *be* somebody).
– Zig Ziglar

Finish well.
– Dr. Billy Graham

The reputation of a thousand years may be determined by the conduct of one hour.
- A Japanese proverb

Difficulties seldom defeat people; lack of faith in themselves usually does it.

We are made to persist. That's how we find out who
we are.
> \- Tobias Wolff

Add up what you have, and you'll find that you
won't sell them for all the gold in the world.
> \- Dale Carnegie

Eating words has never given me indigestion.
> \- Winston Churchill

JUST PLAIN FUNNY

When cannibals ate a missionary, they got a taste of religion.

It's always dullest just before the yawn.

The roundest knight at King Arthur's round table was Sir Cumference. He acquired his size from too much pi.

A fishing rod is a stick with a hook at one end and a fool at the other.

I thought I saw an eye doctor on an Alaskan island, but it turned out to be an optical Aleutian.

She was only a whisky maker, but he loved her still.

A rubber band pistol was confiscated from algebra class because it was a weapon of math disruption.

A flashlight is a case for holding dead batteries.

If a parsley farmer is sued, can they garnish his wages?

Two things bad for the heart: running upstairs and running people down.

The first rule in looking good: don't sneeze in the barber chair.

Better to understand a little, than to misunderstand a lot.

Discover wildlife, have kids.

If everything is under control, you must be moving too slowly.

I'm not one to criticize anyone's spouse, but at least when she got married she got a new dress and a new name.

No matter how much you push the envelope, it'll still be stationery.

A dog gave birth to puppies near the road and was cited for littering.

A grenade thrown into a kitchen in France would result in Linoleum Blownapart.

Two silk worms had a race. They ended up in a tie.

Time flies like an arrow. Fruit flies like a banana.

Two hats were hanging on a hat rack in the hallway. One hat said to the other, "You stay here I'll go on a head."

I wondered why the baseball kept getting bigger. Then it hit me.

A sign on the lawn at a drug rehab center said: "Keep off the Grass."

Sign on the entrance to the hospital delivery room – "Push, Push, Push."

A small boy swallowed some coins and was taken to a hospital. When his grandmother telephoned to ask how he was, the nurse said, "No change yet."

A chicken crossing the road is poultry in motion.

The short fortune-teller who escaped from prison was a small medium at large.

You might be from a small town if:
- Third street is on the edge of town
- They cancel all social events when the gym floor gets re-varnished
- There are only 3 Baptist churches
- You can still eat lunch at the drugstore
- You don't have to signal for a turn because everybody knows where you live
- You're pastor looks like Conway Twiddy
- Two words: Tasty Freeze

The soldier who survived mustard gas and pepper spray is now a seasoned veteran.

LEADERSHIP

Productivity is never an accident. It is always the result of a commitment to excellence, intelligent planning and focused effort.
> - Paul J. Meyer

There is a Hassidic saying, Everyone should carefully observe which way his heart draws him, and then choose that way with all his strength.

As a leader you are either leading the way or in the way.

If you've jumped on the bandwagon, it's probably because you missed the boat.
> - Clyde Hughes

In the past, yesterday's successes provided the wisdom for tomorrow's leaders. What worked in the past was copied, printed, distributed, and applied in the present. Success trickled down as our managers, mentors, and elders passed on their methods and techniques to the next generation. As time went on, however, leaders came to realize the old approaches were not producing the same results. Things had quietly, almost mysteriously, changed. Leaders responded by working harder, longer, and even muttering a prayer or two as they did. They were busy, buried, and falling further behind. They worked harder than ever, with little to show for it. It worked before, but why not now?

- H. Dale Burke

Vision is the ability to see things as they ought to be and can become.

Followers want comfort, stability, and solutions from their leaders, but that's babysitting. Real leaders ask hard questions and knock people out of their comfort zones and then manage the resulting distress.

– Harvard Business Review

Leadership

I can name you the head coach, but I can't name you
the leader. Titles come from above. Leaders are
selected by those under you. They will follow you if
you have a vision and a plan.
>   - Father Hesburgh at Notre Dame
>   to Lou Holtz

People are difficult. Some days I'd like to commit
suicide, but why should I let the rascals outlive me?
>   - Clyde Hughes

The speed of the leader determines the rate of the
pack.

If persistence does trump talent and looks every
time, perhaps that explains why we have so many
untalented leaders.
>   – Clyde Hughes

What pride does:
- Instead of taking responsibility, you blame others. Surely someone else is at fault if things don't work out.
- Instead of being objective, you live in denial. Prideful leaders ignore problems.
- Instead of being open-minded and receptive, you are defensive and guard the sacred cows.
- Instead of flexibility, you have rigidity. "We do it my way or I'm out of here."
- Instead of team spirit, you end up with low morale. The prideful leader inflates himself and deflates others. By taking credit for the successes, the staff becomes disillusioned and leaves.
- Instead of loyalty, you experience high turnover.
- Instead of excellence, pride boasts of greatness but settles for mediocrity.
- Instead of balance, you end up becoming a workaholic. You have to be in control and workers run from control.
- Instead of being connected, you become out of touch with everyone. It's about you and not your constituents.

Leadership

A leader has two important characteristics; first, he is going somewhere; second, he is able to persuade other people to go with him.
> - Maximilien Robespierre

The time to repair the roof is when the sun is shining.
> - John F. Kennedy

If a man has done his best, what else is there?
> – Gen. George S. Patton

You can be a great leader, but it won't happen in a day. Start paying the price now.
> - John Maxwell

We will either find a way or make one.
>
> \- Hannibal, who fought against
> the Romans

There is no doubt that creativity is the most important human resource of all. Without creativity, there would be no progress, and we would be forever repeating the same patterns.
>
> \- Edward de Bono

Every problem has in it the seeds of its own solution. If you don't have any problems, you don't get any seeds.
>
> \- Norman Vincent Peale

Anyone can hold the helm when the sea is calm.
>
> – Johnny Hunt

Unless you try to do something beyond what you have already mastered, you will never grow.
– Ronald E. Osborne

The tragedy of life is what dies inside a man while he lives.
– Albert Einstein

Throw your heart over the fence and the rest will follow.
- Norman Vincent Peale

Nothing happens...but first a dream.
- Carl Sandburg

The two most important leadership issues are vision and will – and neither is related to ability.
– Johnny Hunt

We were surprised, shocked really, to discover the type of leadership required for turning a good company into a great one … good-to-great leaders… are a paradoxical blend of personal humility and professional will.
– Jim Collins, author of "Good to Great"

Men make history, and not the other way around. In periods where there is no leadership, society stands still. Progress occurs when courageous, skillful leaders seize the opportunity to change things for the better.
- Harry Truman

LESSONS OF LIFE

If you get mad at a horse, before you jam the pitchfork into the ground, make sure all four prongs go into the ground and not into your foot. Better yet, just don't get mad.

The greatest lesson in life is to know that even fools are right sometimes.
                            - Winston Churchill

Never question the truth of what you fail to understand, for the world is filled with wonders.
                            - Frederick Buechner, The Sacred
                              Journey

He's mad at the world and seems to believe I created it.
                            - Clyde Hughes

Good philosophy must exist, if for no other reason because bad philosophy needs to be answered.
                    - C. S. Lewis

Statistics show that if you want to avoid poverty in the Unites States, you must do three things: graduate from high school, marry after the age of twenty, and marry before having your first child. Only 8 percent of those who do these three things become poor as adults, whereas 79 percent of poor of poor adults have failed to do these three things.
                    - The Progress Paradox by Gregg Easterbrook

Look twice before crossing a street. Look twice at the sign before entering a rest room.

Hay is heavier once the cow gets through with it.

Speaking of such things, manure is such undesirable stuff, but when your horse throws you, better to land in a pile of soft manure than hard ground.

CATS & TEENAGERS

For all of you with teenagers or who have had teenagers, you probably already know that they have a lot in common with cats:

1. Neither teenagers nor cats turn their heads when you call them by name.

2. No matter what you do for them, it is not enough. Indeed, all human efforts are barely adequate to compensate for the privilege of waiting on them hand and foot.

3. You rarely see a cat walking outside of the house with an adult human being, and it can be safely said that no teenager in his or her right mind wants to be seen in public with his or her parents.

CATS AND TEENAGERS, Cont'd

4. Even if you tell jokes as well as Jay Leno, neither your cat nor your teen will ever crack a smile.

5. No cat or teenager shares your taste in music.

6. Cats and teenagers can lie on the living-room sofa for hours on end without moving, barely breathing.

7. Cats have nine lives. Teenagers live as if they did.

8. Cats and teenagers yawn in exactly the same manner, communicating that ultimate human ecstasy--a sense of complete and utter boredom.

9. Cats and teenagers do not improve anyone's furniture.

10. Cats that are free to roam outside sometimes have been known to return in the middle of the night to deposit a dead animal in your bedroom. Teenagers are not above that sort of behavior.

Remember above all else, put out the food and do not make any sudden moves in their direction. When they make up their minds, they finally will come to you for some affection and comfort; and it will be a triumphant moment for all concerned.

(from Mikey's Funnies)

Lessons of Life

Never loan anything you wouldn't want to give away.

It's hard to make a comeback when you haven't been anywhere.

Never put both feet in your mouth at the same time, because then you won't have a leg to stand on.

Keep your mouth closed, especially when standing up in the back of a truck.

If you throw a rock into a pack of dogs, the one who squeals is likely the one you hit.

When learning to ride a bike, the brake lesson should come before the hill lesson.

Monkeys in India love to yank out a handful of hair.

It is better to be silent and be thought a fool, than to speak and remove all doubt.

Only a fool tests the depth of the water with both feet.
> - An African Proverb

As I grow older I pay less attention to what men say. I just watch what they do.
> - Andrew Carnegie

LIFE'S QUESTIONS

When a chameleon dives into water, is he clear and invisible?

When a turtle loses his shell, is he homeless or naked?

If absolute power corrupts absolutely, does absolute powerlessness make you pure?
                    - Harry Shearer

Isn't Disney World just a people trap operated by a mouse?

If a cow laughed real hard, would milk come out her nose?

How can someone "draw a blank"?

If all those psychics know the winning lottery numbers, why are they all still working?

How much deeper would the ocean be if sponges didn't grow in it?

If the funeral procession is at night, do folks drive with their lights off?

Why are there interstate highways in Hawaii?

Life's Questions

Why do we drive on parkways and park on driveways?

Why does flammable and inflammable mean the same thing?

Why is it that when you transport something by car, it's called a shipment, but when you transport something by ship it's called cargo?

Why does your nose run and your feet smell?

75

MANAGEMENT / ORGANIZATION

The things we fear most in organizations —
fluctuations, disturbances, imbalances — are the
primary sources of creativity.
> - Margaret J. Wheatley

You have to be willing to profoundly question what
you did in the past, and in that sense you have to be
prepared to make yourself vulnerable. That's a hard
thing, but reengineering, whether it be management
or processes, begins here.
> – James Champy

Organizations tend to lose vitality rather than gain it
as time passes.
> – Chuck Swindoll

Think of structure as a verb rather than a noun.
　　　　- Daniel Brown

If I had six hours to chop down a tree, I'd spend the first four sharpening the axe.
　　　　- Abe Lincoln

Too often organization is a good thing gone bad because of our inability to adapt it as needed.
　　　　- Johnny Hunt

Simplify your organizational structure so an eight year old could understand how it operates.
　　　　- Bob Kreitner

Sometimes I get the feeling that the two biggest problems in America today are making ends meet and making meetings end.
– Robert Orben

You can't control your time without scheduling your workday.
– Johnny Hunt

If you can't manage a secretary, then you can't manage a staff or a team of workers or an organization.
– Johnny Hunt

Plan your work for today and every day, then work your plan.
- Norman Vincent Peale

The real cause of paperwork crises is a decision making problem – picking up the same piece of paper five times and putting it down again because you can't decide what to do with it.
– Stephanie Winston

Time is a natural resource – like fuel. When it is abundant, we take it for granted; when it becomes scarce, we search for that extra gallon, regardless of cost. Time is a precious gift – every second, every minute, every day – use it wisely. You cannot pay the cost of losing time.
– Sonny Gann

Managing time is not about managing the clock; it's about managing your life.
– Johnny Hunt.

Schedule time for interruptions.
– Johnny Hunt

Learn how to separate the majors from the minors.
A lot of people don't do well simply because they
major in minor things.
- Jim Rohn

People who are constantly killing time are really
killing their own chances in life. Those who are
destined to become successful are those who make
time and use it wisely.
– Arthur Brisbane

Unlike other resources, time cannot be bought or
sold, borrowed or stolen, stocked up or save,
manufactured, reproduced or modified. All we can
do is make use of it. And whether we used it or not,
it nevertheless slips away.
– Jen-Louis Servan-Scriber.

MARRIAGE / RELATIONSHIPS

By all means, marry. If you get a good wife, you'll become happy; if you get a bad one, you'll become a philosopher.
                    - Socrates

The more tranquil a man becomes, the greater is his success, his influence, his power for good. Calmness of mind is one of the beautiful jewels of wisdom.
                    - James Allen

Whenever you get into a jam, whenever you get into a crisis or an emergency, become the calmest person in the room and you'll be able to figure your way out of it.
                    - Rudy Giuliani

Too many parents tie up their dogs and let their children run loose.

Last week, I stated this woman was the ugliest woman I had ever seen. I have since been visited by her sister, and now wish to withdraw that statement.
- Mark Twain

Ben Franklin discovered electricity in an unusual way. His wife got angry at him and told him to go fly a kite. So that's why we have electric lights.
– Rev. Kermit Gardner

I have found the paradox that if I love until its hurts, then there is no more hurt, but only more love.
– Mother Teresa

My wife has a slight impediment in her speech.
Every now and then she stops to breathe.
> \- Jimmy Durante

A loving person lives in a loving world. A hostile person lives in a hostile world. Everyone you meet is your mirror.
> \- Ken Keyes

I was married by a judge. I should have asked for a jury.
> \- Groucho Marx

We must learn to manage conflict: We can never resolve differences.
> – H. Norman Wright

Forgiveness is admitting we are all alike.

Kind words can be short and sweet but their echoes go forever.
> - Mother Teresa

One of the greatest gifts you can give anyone is the gift of attention.
> - Jim Rohn

Love is a canvas furnished by Nature and embroidered by imagination.
> – Voltaire

All that we love deeply become a part of us.
> - Helen Keller

If all men are imperfect, part of the reason is that women get to define perfection.
> - Clyde Hughes

MILITARY WISDOM
(Quoted in IPCC LIFE)

"A slipping gear could let your M203 grenade launcher fire when you least expect it. That would make you quite unpopular in what's left of your unit."
> - Army's magazine of preventive maintenance

"Aim toward the enemy."
> - Instruction printed on U.S. rocket launcher

"When the pin is pulled, Mr. Grenade is not our friend."
> - U.S. Marine Corps

"If the enemy is in range, so are you."
                    - Infantry Journal

"It is generally inadvisable to eject directly over the area you just bombed."
                    - U.S. Air Force Manual

"Whoever said the pen is mightier than the sword obviously never encountered automatic weapons."
                    - General MacArthur

"Try to look unimportant; they may be low on ammo."
                    - Infantry Journal

"You, you, and you . . . panic. The rest of you, come with me."
- U.S. Marine Corp Gunnery Sergeant

"Tracers work both ways."
- U.S. Army Ordnance

"Don't ever be the first, don't ever be the last, and don't ever volunteer to do anything."
- U.S. Navy swabbie

"If your attack is going too well, you're walking into an ambush."
- Infantry Journal

"No combat-ready unit has ever passed inspection."
- Joe Gay

"Any ship can be a minesweeper ... once."
- Unknown source

"Never tell the platoon sergeant you have nothing to do."
- Unknown marine recruit

"Don't draw fire; it irritates the people around you."
- Your buddies

"If you see a bomb technician running, follow him."
- U.S.A.F. Ammo Troop

When in England at a fairly large conference, Colin Powell was asked by the Archbishop of Canterbury if our plans for Iraq were just an example of "empire building" by George Bush. He answered by saying, "Over the years, the United States has sent many of its fine young men and women into great peril to fight for freedom beyond our borders. The only amount of land we have ever asked for in return is enough to bury those that did not return."

Bravery is being the only one who knows you're afraid.

- David Hackworth

MONEY

My luck is so bad that if I bought a cemetery, people would stop dying.
> \- Rodney Dangerfield

Money can't buy you happiness. But it does bring you a more pleasant form of misery.
> \- Spike Milligan

Wealth is always a relative matter: the more wealth you have, the more relatives you hear from.
> \- Old Union Reminder

Money doesn't change men, it merely unmasks them. If a man is naturally selfish or arrogant or greedy, the money brings that out - that is all.
> \- Henry Ford

Money

If your outgo exceeds your income then your upkeep will be your downfall.

If you don't have payments, you will have money.
            - Dave Ramsey

If you'll live like no one else, then one day you can live like no one else.
            – Dave Ramsey

You can't borrow your way out of debt.
            – Dave Ramsey

God will give more TO you if He can get more THRU you – Caller on Dave Ramsey's Radio Talk Show

One thing a child outgrows in a hurry: your pocketbook

If only the people who worry about their liabilities would think about the riches they do possess, they would stop worrying.
                    - Dale Carnegie

America's safety net for the poor has been turned into a hammock.

What's a good investment? Go home from work early and spend the afternoon throwing a ball around with your son.
                    - Ben Stein

MOTHERHOOD/WOMEN

A mother is the only person on earth who can divide her love among ten children and each child still have all her love.

It is the atmosphere created primarily by the mother that makes a home worthwhile.
- J.R. Bookhoff

There was never a child so lovely but his mother was glad to get him asleep.
- Ralph Waldo Emerson

The mother's heart is the child's schoolroom.
- Henry Ward Beecher

If I cannot give my children a perfect mother I can at least given them more of the one they've got—and make that one more loving. I will be available, I will take time to listen, time to play, time to be home when they arrive from school, time to counsel and encourage.
                    - Ruth Bell Graham

A suburban mother's role is to deliver children obstetrically once, and by car forever after.
                    - Peter DeVries

There's no way to be a perfect mother and a million ways to be a good one.
                    - Jill Churchill

The phrase "working mother" is redundant.
                    - Jane Sellman

One woman I know really dresses to kill and cooks the same way.

I usually take my wife to a night club. It's the only place still open by the time she finishes dressing.

I only listen to my wife when she talks in her sleep.

Definition: Homely woman – all dressed up and no face to go.

Women are unpredictable. You never know how they are going to manage to get their own way.

A woman doesn't really make a fool of a man – she merely gives him opportunity to develop his natural capacities.

I learned about women the hard way; I married one.

A woman never forgets her age once she decides on it.

OLD AGE

I can't imagine a wise old person who can't laugh!
- Erik H. Erikson

Live every day like it's your last. 'Cause one day
you're going to be right.
- Ray Charles

The older I get, the better I used to be.
- Lee Trevino

Those who love deeply never grow old; they may
die of old age, but they die young.
- Benjamin Franklin

A 50 year old woman's hair was turning white so she dyed it black. When her husband cam home from work she said to him, "Do I look 10 years younger?" He said, "No, but your hair does."
– Rev. Kermit Gardner

You're never too old to learn – but that's no reason to keep putting it off!

In my day, we didn't have water. We had to smash together our own hydrogen and oxygen atoms.

Back in my day, 60 Minutes wasn't just a bunch of gray-haired liberal 80-year-old guys. It was a bunch of gray-haired liberal 60-year-old guys.

Old Age

If it doesn't hurt, it doesn't work!

In my day, we didn't have virtual reality. If a one-eyed razorback barbarian warrior was chasing you with an ax, you just had to hope you could outrun him. (The Daily Dilly)

Games for older dads:
1. Sag, you're it
2. Pin the toupee on the bald guy
3. Spin the bottle of Mylanta
4. Musical recliners

Life begins at 40 – but so do fallen arches, arthritis, faulty eyesight and the tendency to tell a story to the same person three or four times.
    - William Feather

HOW TO STAY YOUNG (seen in IPCC Life, edited by Bishop Rev. Clyde Hughes)

1. Throw out nonessential numbers. This includes age, weight and height. Let the doctors worry about them. That is why you pay 'them.'

2. Keep only cheerful friends. Others pull you down. Use de-grouching powder daily.

3. Keep learning. Rediscover the world of reading. Learn more about the computer, crafts, gardening, whatever. Never let the brain idle. 'An idle mind is the devil's workshop.' Keep his aid, Alzheimer's, at bay.

4. Rediscover the child within. Enjoy the simple things. All of life is awe-inspiring!

5. Laugh often, long and loud. Laugh until you gasp for breath.

6. Tears happen. Endure, grieve, and move on. The only human who is with us our entire life, is ourselves. When you die, you'll be really dead. Be totally ALIVE while you are alive.

7. Surround yourself with what you love, whether it's family, pets, keepsakes, music, plants or hobbies.

8. Cherish your health: If it is good, preserve it. If it is unstable, improve it. If it is beyond what you can improve, get help.

HOW TO STAY YOUNG, cont'd

9. Don't take guilt trips. Acknowledge sin and take it to God. Take a trip to the mall, even to the next county; to a foreign country but NOT to where guilt is. Get forgiven and leave it.

10. Tell the people you love that you love them, at every opportunity.

11. Keep God at the center of your life and ground-zero of every activity. It was He who brought you into this world and He will be your only concern as you depart it.

Middle age: when you're sitting at home on Saturday night and the telephone rings and you hope it isn't for you.
                    - Ogden Nash

Back in the 1970s we didn't have the space shuttle to get all excited about. We had to settle for men walking on the crummy moon.

Old Age

In my day, we didn't have days. There was only
time for work, time for prayer and time for sleep.
The sheriff would go around and tell everyone when
to change.

In my day, we didn't have hand-held calculators.
We had to do addition on our fingers. To subtract,
we had to have some fingers amputated.

Middle age is when a narrow waist and a broad
mind begin to change places.
                    - Glen Dorenbush

Fitness video for older men: "Remotes of Steel"

Old Age

A Poem

Mirror, mirror on the wall,
Can this be me, wrinkles and all?

Mirror, mirror on the wall,
I'm just too young for grey hair at all!

Mirror, mirror on the wall,
That's not the body I remember at all!

Mirror, mirror on the wall,
Where I left my mind – I can't recall!

A youthful figure is something you get when you
ask a woman her age.

Birthdays are good for you. The more you have, the
longer you live.

I must be getting absent-minded. Whenever I complain that things aren't what they used to be, I always forget to include myself.
                    - George Burns

He's so old that when he orders a three minute egg, they ask for the money up front!
                    - Milton Berle

The Cardiologist's Diet: If it tastes good, spit it out!

ONE LINERS

Always try to drive so that your license will expire before you do.

A committee is a group that keeps minutes and wastes hours.

Alarm Clock: device to wake adults who have no children.

My girlfriend is very temperamental: 80% temper and the rest mental.

My wife has two mink coats. I surprised her with the first and she surprised me with the second.

I got this dog for my wife. I should have made that trade years ago.

The noblest of all dogs is the hot dog. It feeds the hand that bites it.

I'm not saying he drank a lot in college, but he did graduate Magna Cum Loaded.

French fries stay in your mouth for a few minutes, in your stomach a few hours and on your hips forever.

If I ever win the girl of my dreams, what will I do with my wife?

It must have been love at first sight. If I'd taken a second look, I'd have turned and run.

For every man over 65 there are 7 women. Of course, by then it's too late.

My uncle was so lazy he'd put coffee grounds in his mustache and drink hot water.

I used to beat up all the kids on my block except the Jones's. They were boys.

Tonight I'd like to sing a medley of my hit song.

I'm always being blamed when things go wrong. Even when I was a baby they were always pinning things on me.

The salary we used to dream of is the one we can't live on today.

Adam had no mother-in-law. That's how we know he lived in paradise.

The only instrument I play is second fiddle at home.

Weight loss slogan: A word to the wide is sufficient.

My son got the highest marks of any kid who flunked.

College presidents never die, they just lose their faculties.

A word to the wise may be sufficient, but a whole book won't help the stupid.

POSITIVE THINKING

Nobody knows the trouble I've seen. But they ought
to as much as I tell them.
                              - Clyde Hughes

I've always been the opposite of a paranoid. I
operate as if everyone is part of a plot to enhance my
well-being.
                              - Stan Dale

All my life I have tried to pluck a thistle and plant a
flower wherever the flower would grow in thought
and mind.

Ultimately, the only power to which man should
aspire is that which he exercises over himself.
- Elie Wiesel

I have enjoyed life a lot more by saying yes than by
saying no.
- Richard Branson

Blessed is he who expects nothing, for he shall never
be disappointed.
- Benjamin Franklin

The only limit to our realization of tomorrow will be
our doubts of today.
- Franklin Delano Roosevelt

You become positive by deciding in advance that you will always choose the most resourceful response to any given set of circumstances.
- Tommy Newberry

Those who say nothing but good can happen when we welcome the undocumented alien has never talked to an American Indian.
- Clyde Hughes

People constantly underestimate their abilities, and it is the responsibility of parents, coaches, and teachers to raise their self-image and expectations.
- Lou Holtz

Optimism is essential to achievement and it is also the foundation of courage and of true progress.
- Nicholas Murray Butler

Believe you are defeated, believe it long enough, and it is likely to become a fact.
> - Norman Vincent Peale

Accept that some days you're the pigeon, and some days you're the statue.

Always keep your words soft and sweet, just in case you have to eat them.

Always read stuff that will make you look good if you die in the middle of it.

The quickest way to embalm your future is to lose your enthusiasm

Drive carefully. It's not only cars that can be recalled by their maker.

If you can't be kind, at least have the decency to be vague.

It may be that your sole purpose in life is simply to be kind to others.

It's the second mouse that gets the cheese.

When everything's coming your way, you're in the wrong lane.

Some mistakes are too much fun to only make once.

We could learn a lot from crayons--some are sharp, some are pretty, some are dull, and some have weird names, but they all have to live in the same box.

A truly happy person is one who can enjoy the scenery on a detour.

Our duty as men is to proceed as if limits to our ability did not exist.
                              - Pierre Teihard de Chardin

If only the people who worry about their liabilities would think about the riches they do possess, they would stop worrying.
                              - Dale Carnegie

Your own resolution to success is more important than any other one thing.
  - Abraham Lincoln

Some people act like they've been baptized in vinegar and given a transfusion of pickle juice.
  - Clyde Hughes

The probability that we may fail in the struggle ought not to deter us from the support of a cause we believe to be just.
  - Abraham Lincoln

PREACHERS / PREACHING

The secret of a good sermon is to have a good beginning and a good ending; and to have the two as close together as possible.
                    - George Burns

Some sermons are as thin as the homeopathic soup that was made by boiling the shadow of a pigeon that had been starved to death!
                    - Abe Lincoln

Justice is giving someone what they deserve.
Mercy is not giving someone what they deserve.
Grace is giving someone what they do not deserve.
                    - H. Dale Burke

No grace is stronger than humility.
> \- Richard Sibbes, 17th Century
> minister

A Bible and a newspaper in every house, a good school in every district - - all studied and appreciated as they merit - - are the principal support of virtue, morality and civil liberty.
> \- Benjamin Franklin

A patriot without religion in my estimation is a great a paradox as an honest man without the fear of God. Is it possible that he whom no moral obligations bind can have any real good will toward men? Can he be a patriot who, by an openly vicious conduct, is undermining the very bonds of Society?...The scriptures tell us "righteousness exalts a nation."
> \- Abigail Adams

A Bible is worth all other books which have ever
been printed.
- Patrick Henry

Here is my creed: I believe in one God, the creator of
the universe. that He governs it by His providence,
that he ought to be worshipped.
- Benjamin Franklin

A Sunday school teacher asked, 'Johnny, do you
think Noah did a lot of fishing when he was on the
Ark?'
'No,' replied Johnny. 'How could he, with just two
worms.'

It is when people forget God that tyrants forge their
chains.
- Patrick Henry

I have carefully examined the evidences of the Christian religion and if I were sitting as a juror upon its authenticity I would unhesitatingly give my verdict in its favor. I can prove its truth as clearly as any proposition ever submitted to the mind of man.
-Alexander Hamilton

A Sunday school teacher was telling her class the story of the Good Samaritan. She asked the class, 'If you saw a person lying on the roadside, all wounded and bleeding, what would you do?' A thoughtful little girl broke the hushed silence, 'I think I'd throw up.'

TEAMWORK

There's no limit to what a man can do or where he can go if he doesn't mind who gets the credit.
- Ronald Reagan

A team filled with players who believe in one another, and who believe they can win, who are willing to work hard and do the things necessary to become successful: that is a winning team regardless of their record.
- Lou Holtz

My driving belief is great teamwork is the only way to reach our ultimate moments.
– Pat Riley

The gap between good teams and championship teams is very small.
>   – Don Shula

The great strength of the church is that people don't work for a living – they work for a cause.
>   – Peter Drucker

Execution is about paying attention to details. If a team looks sloppy in the huddle, it will look sloppy during the play.
>   - Lou Holtz

I learned that a team goes through four stages: first, they have to learn how to compete; then they have to learn how to win; after that, they have to learn how to handle winning; then and only then are they ready to win championships.
>   - Lou Holtz

UP TIME

If you see injustice, STAND UP
If something needs to be said, SPEAK UP
If you make an appointment, SHOW UP
If you make a mistake, FESS UP
If you're overstepping, BACK UP
If you get behind, CATCH UP
If they knock you down, GET UP
If you're out of line, STRAIGHTEN UP
When your boss instructs, KEEP UP
When your elders speak, LISTEN UP
When your teachers teach, SIT UP
When your preachers preach, WAKE UP
When your country calls, MAN UP
Ladies too... WOMAN UP
When the fight is over, MAKE UP
If you're being hard, EASE UP
If your heart is closed, OPEN UP
If you want to buy something, SAVE UP--
It's not an entitlement, so SHUT UP!
If you make a mess, CLEAN IT UP
If you drop trash, PICK IT UP
If a car is waiting for you to walk across the street,
SPEED IT UP
If you're cold busted, GIVE IT UP
If people fall down, HELP THEM UP--
Not the government, YOU STEP UP
If idiots start fighting, BREAK IT UP

UP TIME, Cont'd

If the music is wholesome, TURN IT UP
If the message is poisonous, THROW IT UP
If your words are vulgar, CLAM IT UP
If your words encourage, KEEP IT UP
If your pants are baggy, PULL THEM UP
If the belt's too loose, CINCH IT UP
If your fly is down, ZIP IT UP
If you're dressed half naked, COVER IT UP
If you can't afford stuff, PASS IT UP--
No "bailouts" folks, PONY UP
If you made a promise, you BACK IT UP
And you can take your whining and PACK IT UP
It's called personal responsibility, so TAKE IT UP
This country was founded on it, you can LOOK IT
UP
It's the American way people, so TURN IT UP
Because when life gets boring, you SHAKE IT UP
When life is good, you SOAK IT UP
When life's unfair, you SUCK IT UP
When life is funny, you can YUCK IT UP
When life is sad, just LOOK STRAIGHT UP
And life's too short people, so LIVE IT UP!

– UptimeAmerica.com reported in IPCC Life

WINNING & LOSING

Productivity is never an accident. It is always the result of a commitment to excellence, intelligent planning and focused effort.
                    - Paul J. Meyer

Let me tell you the secret that has led me to my goal: my strength lies solely in my tenacity.
                    – Louis Pasteur

In any project the important factor is your belief. Without belief there can be no successful outcome.
                    - William James

If you worried about falling off the bike, you'd never get on.
>   - Lance Armstrong

Throughout history, the most extraordinary acts of genius have often come in the depths of turmoil.
>   - Lou Holtz

Success is knowing your purpose in life, growing to reach your maximum potential, and sowing seeds that benefit others.

If you're big enough for your dream then your dream is not big enough for you.
>   - Erwin McManus

You can use most any measure when you're speaking of success. You can measure it in a fancy home, expensive care or dress. But the measure of your real success is one you cannot spend – It is the way your child describes you when talking to a friend.

— Martin Baxbaum

If we're going to be successful, we have to get rid of excuses for why we can't win.

— Lou Holtz

To be a real winner, you have to stop doing the stuff that's not good for you.

— Jim Allen

Parking meters should remind us that we lose money standing still.

— Bert Kruse

Happiness lies in the joy of achievement and the thrill of creative effort.
> - Franklin D. Roosevelt

Winners vs Losers

The Winner is always part of the answer.
The Loser is always part of the problem.
The winner always has a program.
The Loser always has an excuse.
The Winner says, "Let me do it for you."
The Loser says, "That's not my job."
The Winner sees an answer for every problem.
The Loser sees a problem for every answer.
The Winner sees a green near every sand trap.
The Loser sees two or three sand traps near every
        green.
The Winner says, "It may be difficult, but it's
        possible."
The Loser says, "It may be possible, but it's too
        difficult."

So BE A WINNER!

If you have the will to win, you have achieved half your success; if you don't, you have achieved half your failure.
                    – David Ambrose

It's critical to have goals in life, and to work as hard as you can to achieve those goals, but in the end, the Lord works in mysterious ways. Hard times will come. They always do. But when it happens, remember that deep faith, hard work, and an unwavering commitment to your goals will turn today's tragedy into tomorrow's triumphs.
                    - Lou Holtz

The harder you work, the harder it is to surrender.
                    - Vince Lombardi

One who fears failure limits his worth. Failure is the opportunity to begin again more intelligently.
                    - Henry Ford

Excuses come only out of the losing locker room. Winners don't need to make excuses, and they don't have time because they are too busy finding solutions.
>   - Lou Holtz

Practice does not make perfect. Perfect practice makes perfect.
>   - Lou Holtz

A great pleasure in life is doing what others have said you could not do.

Miracles are not a contradiction of nature. They are only in contradiction to what we know of nature.
>   - Augustine

The will to practice is greater than the will to win.
- Tom Landry

The difference between a successful person and others is not a lack of strength, not a lack of knowledge, but rather in a lack of will.
- Vince Lombardi

Nothing in the world could take the place of persistence. Nothing in the world is more common that unsuccessful men with talent.
- Calvin Coolidge

Success is on the far side of failure.
- Thomas Watson

It's a good day when you can laugh at your failures.
– Johnny Hunt

Nothing breeds future successes like present successes.
- Vince Lombardi

When you affirm big, believe big, and pray big, big things happen.
- Norman Vincent Peale

A lifetime of self-doubt is far more painful and damaging than shooting for the stars and falling short.
- David Jeremiah

Eighty-five percent of the reason you get a job, keep that job, and move ahead in that job has to do with your people skills and people knowledge.
- Cavett Robert

There is but one cause of human failure. And that is man's lack of faith in his true self.
- William James

A life making mistakes is not only more honorable, but in the long run we get no more than we have been willing to risk giving.
- Sheldon Kopp

A window of opportunity won't open itself.
- Dave Weinbaum

A single sacrifice seldom produces success.

A problem, at its core, is really just an opportunity to learn and explore.
              - Stephen Coleman

5816828R0

Made in the USA
Charleston, SC
06 August 2010